NATIONAL GEOGRAPHIC

T0045067

Kids

Care for the Earth

Gare Thompson

PICTURE CREDITS
Cover (clockwise) David Woodfall/Stone, Frank Siteman/Stone, Michael Newman/PhotoEdit, Lori Adamski Peek/Stone, Steve Skjold/PhotoEdit; pages 1, 16 (top), 19 (inset), 25, 27, Photodisc; page 3 PhotoEdit; page 3 (left), 5 (top) Gerard del Vecchio/Stone; pages 3 (center), 7 Chad Ehlers/Stone Images; pages 3 (right), 26 (bottom) David Woodfall/Stone; pages 4-5 Tom Bol/Outside Images; pages 5 (center), 24 Jose Azel/Aurora; page 6 (top) Deborah Davis/PhotoEdit, (bottom) Gary Holscher/Stone; page 8 (top & bottom) James P. Blair/National Geographic Society, Image Collection, (center) Rainbow; pages 9, 10, 18 (center), 28 (bottom) National Geographic Society, Image Collection; page 11 (top) George Mobley/National Geographic Society, Image Collection; pages 12 (top), 22 Mary Kate Denny/PhotoEdit; page 12 (bottom) Jean Shapiro Cantu; page 13 James P. Blair/National Geographic Society, Image Collection; page 14 (top) Raymond K. Gehman/National Geographic Society, Image Collection, (center) Denis J. Finley/National Geographic Society, Image Collection, (bottom) Jodi Cobb/National Geographic Society, Image Collection; page 16 (bottom) Charles Kennard/Stock Boston; page 17 © Alan Towse/Bettmann/COR-BIS; page 18 (top) James A. Sugar/National Geographic Society, Image Collection, (bottom) Medford Taylor/National Geographic Society, Image Collection; page 19 Joel Sartore/National Geographic Society, Image Collection, page 20 John Lee/Stock Boston; page 21 Todd Gipstein/National Geographic Society, Image Collection; page 23 Steve Skjold/PhotoEdit, (inset) Henryk Kaiser/Leo de Wys Stock Photo Agency; page 28 (top) Dick S. Durrance/National Geographic Society, Image Collection; page 29 Julie Marotte/Stock Boston; back cover Deborah Davis/PhotoEdit, Myrleen Cate/Stone, © VCG/FPG, © Ken Chernus/FPG, Howard Kingsnorth/Stone

Diagrams
Stephen R. Wagner (pages 11 &15)

Produced through the worldwide resources of the National Geographic Society, John M. Fahey, Jr., President and Chief Executive Officer; Gilbert M. Grosvenor, Chairman of the Board; Nina D. Hoffman, Executive Vice President and President, Books and Education Publishing Group

PREPARED BY NATIONAL GEOGRAPHIC SCHOOL PUBLISHING
Ericka Markman, Senior Vice President and President Children's Books and Education Publishing Group; Steve Mico, Vice President, Editorial Director; Marianne Hiland, Executive Editor; Anita Schwartz, Project Editor; Tara Peterson, Editorial Assistant; Jim Hiscott, Design Manager; Linda McKnight, Art Director; Diana Bourdrez, Anne Whittle, Photo Research; Matt Wascavage, Manager of Publishing Services; Sean Philpotts, Production Manager; Jane Ponton, Production Artist.

MANUFACTURING AND QUALITY MANAGEMENT
Christopher A. Liedel, Chief Financial Officer; Phillip L. Schlosser, Director; Clifton M. Brown III, Manager.

PROGRAM DEVELOPMENT
Gare Thompson Associates, Inc.

BOOK DESIGN
3r1 Group

Published by the National Geographic Society
1145 17th Street, N.W.
Washington, D.C. 20036-4688

ISBN: 0-7922-8675-8

Sixth Printing March, 2018
Printed in the United States of America.

Contents

Earth's Natural Resources................page 4

Chapter 1.....................................page 7
Using Earth's Resources

Chapter 2 ....page 13
The Changing Earth

Chapter 3 ....page 19
Protecting Earth's Resources

Chapter 4....................................page 23
Kids Take Action

Groups to Contact.........................page 30

Glossary ....page 31

Index ....page 32

Earth's Natural Resources

We all need water to drink, land to grow food and build shelters, and air to breathe. But in the future will we have enough water, land, and air? How can we make sure we do? What actions can you take to help care for the Earth?

Our Earth is filled with many useful things found in nature. These things are called **natural resources.**

Some of our natural resources are

- plants
- water
- land
- air
- minerals
- fuels

We use minerals, such as copper, silver, and quartz, to make wires, jewelry, computers, and so many other products. We burn fuels, like oil and gasoline, to heat our homes and power our cars.

But what happens to natural resources after we use them?

There are two kinds of natural resources on Earth. Resources that can be replaced or replace themselves are called **renewable resources.** Resources that are gone after we use them are called **nonrenewable resources.**

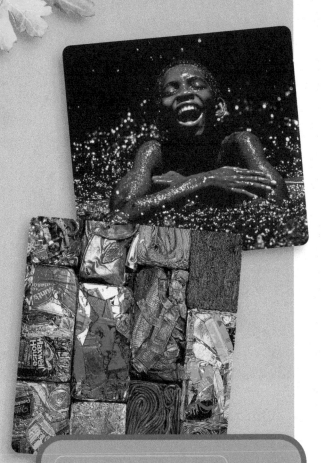

Renewable Resources

- Land can be renewed by adding fertilizer to the soil or by changing the crops grown on it.
- Trees can be replanted.
- Water is renewed whenever it rains or snows.

Nonrenewable Resources

- Minerals that are mined and used cannot be replaced.
- Fuels that are burned and used for energy cannot be replaced.

Our renewable natural resources—water, land, and air—will not last forever if we don't care for them. We have to learn to **conserve**, or protect, these resources. We have to learn to manage them wisely.

For most of us, water seems like a never-ending resource. It pours out of the tap whenever we need some. As the world population grows, more and more people are using water. Conserving our water helps ensure that future generations will still have clean, usable water.

We need clean air to breathe. Our lawmakers have passed laws to help keep our air clean. But many people are trying to find their own ways to keep our air clean and healthy. Some people ride bikes, walk, or take buses or subways instead of driving.

CHAPTER 1

Using Earth's Resources

Water, land, and air are important natural resources. We use these resources every day. We depend on them for life. Think about the many ways people depend on Earth's resources.

We use water to
- wash and clean
- drink
- water plants and gardens
- swim and fish
- travel from place to place

We use air to
- breathe and support life

We use land to
- plant flower gardens
- grow food crops
- grow trees to make paper and wood products
- build homes
- do recreational sports, such as camping and hiking

How do you use these resources? How do you think businesses and industries use these resources?

Fun FACTS

- People drink over 16,000 gallons (60,565 liters) of water during their lifetime.
- Five tons of topsoil spread over one acre is only as thick as a dime.
- The average person takes about 20,000 breaths a day.

Businesses and industries—large and small—are an important part of our country's **economy.** The economy is the way a country produces and uses goods, services, and natural resources. The United States is rich in natural resources. Here are some ways industries use these resources.

Transportation

Farming

Timber Harvesting

Water

- Huge freighters transport, or carry, goods from one part of the world to another on our waterways.
- **Hydroelectric plants** use water to make electricity. Some factories depend on these plants for the power to run their machinery.
- Farmers use water to **irrigate** their crops.

Land

- Farmers use land to grow food and plants like cotton and to raise animals.
- Highways and train tracks are built on the land. Industries transport their goods from place to place on highways and train tracks.
- Companies mine minerals from the land. Industries depend on minerals to **manufacture** products.
- Foresters grow and harvest trees to make paper, furniture, and homes.

Air

- The transportation industry depends on air to fly planes, jets, and hot air balloons.
- The communications and entertainment industries use the airwaves. Most of the sounds we hear travel through the air.

Renewable Resources

Water, land, and air are renewable resources. They renew themselves through cycles. *These cycles ensure that these resources can be renewed or replaced over time.*

Water

Plants, animals, and people need water to live. Water is the most common substance on Earth, yet our supply of usable water is limited.

Water covers more than 70 percent of the Earth's surface. About 97 percent of the water on Earth is in the oceans, which are salty. Only 3 percent is fresh, and most of that water is ice. We need fresh water to drink and to grow crops.

Today we have as much water as the dinosaurs did! The water on Earth replaces itself through the water cycle.

Take a Closer LOOK

The Water Cycle

As the air cools, the vapor condenses, or changes back into a liquid.

Condensation

Precipitation

Water vapor rises and is carried by the air.

Water returns to the earth as rain, snow, or other precipitation.

Evaporation

Some water seeps into the ground. Some water returns to the oceans.

The sun heats water in the soil, rivers, lakes, and oceans. The water evaporates, and turns to water vapor, a gas.

Land

An important part of land is its soil. Plants need soil to grow. People and animals need plants for food.

Soil generally has three layers. The top layer is the most important to plants. This layer is rich in **nutrients,** or plant food. It is called topsoil. The richer the soil, the better plants grow. The diagram shows the layers of soil.

How Soil is Formed

Rain, ice, and other natural forces break down rocks.

Organisms living on the rocks die and decay.

Sand and silt forms.

Soil begins to form from rocks and decaying plants and animals.

As soil develops, the top level becomes deep enough to support plant roots.

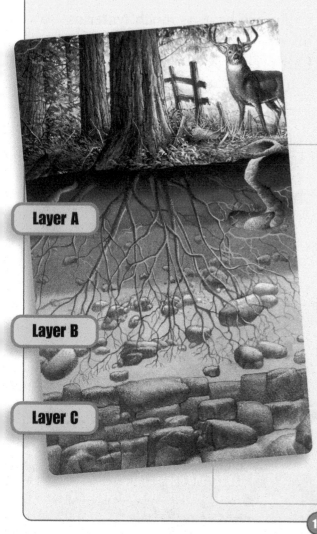

Layer A

Layer B

Layer C

Soil's Three Layers

Layer A is topsoil. Topsoil is alive with roots and tiny living things, such as bacteria, fungi, and worms. When these living things die, they decay, or rot. They turn into the nutrients that make the soil rich and healthy.

Layer B is the second layer. It contains a lot of clay. Plants and animals have a difficult time getting through this hard layer.

Layer C is the third layer. It is made of broken rock. At the bottom is solid rock that turns into the two layers above it.

Air

We all need air to breathe. Air is a mixture of gases. Two of these gases are **oxygen** and **carbon dioxide**. It is the oxygen in the air that we need to live.

Oxygen is renewed through the oxygen-carbon dioxide cycle. The diagram below shows how oxygen in the air is renewed.

The Oxygen-Carbon Dioxide Cycle

1. Plants use light to make their own food. This process is called photosynthesis.
2. During photosynthesis plants take in carbon dioxide and give off oxygen.
3. Oxygen is released into the air.
4. People and animals breathe in oxygen. They breathe out carbon dioxide.

OXYGEN

PHOTOSYNTHESIS

RESPIRATION

CARBON DIOXIDE

People all over the world have been celebrating Earth Day each year since 1970.

Earth Watch

People have cut down almost two-thirds of the original forests on Earth to clear the land for other uses.

Long ago, most people did not worry about natural resources. The rivers, lakes, and oceans were clean. People could find plenty of rich land to farm. There seemed to be an endless supply of natural resources.

But today many more people live in our world. We are rapidly using up or **polluting** our resources. Today we need to find ways to protect or replace our resources.

CHAPTER 2

The Changing Earth

People change the Earth by not taking care of its resources. We waste resources. We also pollute them. We can't drink or wash with polluted water. We can't farm land that has been polluted. We can't breathe air that has been polluted.

Earth Watch

Did you know that the average American throws away 4.3 pounds (2 kilograms) of trash each day?

Water Pollution

Land Pollution

Air Pollution

How is water polluted?

- Factories dump chemicals into rivers, lakes, and streams.
- People throw trash and garbage into the water.
- Farmers use **pesticides** and fertilizers. These chemicals run off the land into the water.
- Untreated waste is dumped into the water.
- Tankers have accidents and oil spills into the waters.

How is land polluted?

- People litter.
- Farmers spray pesticides onto crops.
- Waste materials, such as old cars or paints and cleaning products, are left in trash dumps.
- Factories have industrial accidents, such as chemical spills.

How is air polluted?

- Cars, buses, and trucks burn fuels. Wastes from burning fuels pollute the air.
- Homes and power plants burn coal, oil, or gas for energy.
- Factories give off toxic, or poisonous, smoke.
- People use aerosol cans.

People Waste Resources

People waste water, land, and air. We leave water running when we are not using it. We take long showers. A 5-minute shower uses 25-35 gallons (95-132 liters) of water. Think how much water you would be wasting if you took a 20-minute shower!

We waste land resources by cutting down trees without replacing them. We farm the same land for many years. If improperly managed, these farmlands can use up nutrients in the soil. Then the land becomes barren and crops cannot grow on it.

We waste air by filling it with smoke. Smoking or burning fires without good ventilation, or air circulation, dirties the air. By not smoking, people can keep the air cleaner.

The Greenhouse Effect

In recent years scientists have become very concerned about the **greenhouse effect.** There are gases in the Earth's atmosphere that act like the glass in a greenhouse. They let the sunlight in, but they don't let the sun's heat out. Greenhouse gases come from burning fossil fuels (coal, oil) used by industries, cars, and trucks. These gases are increasing.

Most scientists are worried that as these gases increase, the Earth will get too warm. This condition is called global warming. If the Earth does grow warmer, the ice at the North and South poles will begin to melt. Then our oceans will spill over low-lying coastal areas. World leaders are trying to find ways to reduce greenhouse gases. The diagram below shows the greenhouse effect.

Ozone Layer

The **ozone layer** is a thin layer of gas in the upper atmosphere. The ozone layer protects people and plants from the dangerous rays of the sun. Some refrigerators, air conditioners, and aerosol cans release chemicals into the air. These chemicals break down the ozone layer. As the ozone layer breaks down, it lets in dangerous sun rays. These rays can be very harmful to people, plants, and animals.

Deforestation

Deforestation, or cutting down forest trees, also harms our natural resources. Deforestation hurts the air because trees take in carbon dioxide and return oxygen to the air. Deforestation also hurts the land because trees stop wind and water from blowing away the topsoil. Without trees, land can become barren. Deforestation also destroys the homes of many wild animals.

As the population grows, more land is needed. So more trees are cut down to clear the land to build places for people to live, work, and go to school.

Can you think of ways we can protect our forests?

Trash

Trash is all the unwanted things that we throw away. We throw away food, paper, old clothes, and plastic and metal containers. Some things, such as food, decay and help the soil. Other things, such as plastic and metal, do not. Plastic and metal take a long time to decay.

Earth Watch

Only two places that people have built on Earth can be seen clearly from space: the Great Wall of China and the Fresh Kills Landfill on Staten Island, New York.

Our trash often ends up in **landfills**. Landfills are pits where trash is dumped. A good landfill has a waterproof liner. The liner keeps liquids from leaking into nearby water. The landfill should also have pipes to pump liquids to a treatment plant. Another set of pipes should collect gases.

Acid Rain

When certain chemicals combine in the air, they can make **acid rain**. Cars release nitric oxide. Factories release nitric oxide and sulfur dioxide. These gases combine with water vapor to form sulfuric and nitric acid, or acid rain. This acid rain then falls to Earth.

Acid rain harms water, land, and air. For example, some lakes have become lifeless because of acid rain. The acid rain poisoned every living thing in these lakes including all fish and plants.

At landfills, bulldozers compact the trash, or make it smaller by squeezing it together. Full land-fills are sealed with a cap of soil and clay. Problems can happen if liquids leak into water supplies or if gases escape. These liquids and gases can make people, plants, and animals sick.

When Nature Strikes

Natural disasters, such as earthquakes and floods, also change Earth's resources. These changes affect our future.

Earthquakes

Earthquakes are natural land disasters caused by a sudden breaking and shifting of rock far beneath the Earth's surface.

Drought

Sometimes, the weather stays dry for long periods, causing droughts. During a drought, the water supply in an area dries up. Without water to drink, animals will die. Without water, soil becomes dry and sandy.

Floods

When it rains too much, rivers and streams rise and overflow onto land. Severe floods can cause widespread damage.

Protecting Earth's Resources

Are you ready to take action to protect planet Earth? You may think this sounds like an impossible mission, but one person can make a difference. You can begin by taking some small, but important, first steps.

Water

Here are some tips for conserving water.

- Take shorter showers.
- Run the dishwasher only when it is full.
- Limit your use of water during hot, dry spells.

You can also volunteer to help others who are trying to protect the local water supply. See if there is a group in your neighborhood that has "adopted" a nearby pond or stream. Help them out on clean-up days.

What can you do to conserve or protect our water supply?

Earth Watch

The average home in the United States uses 107,000 gallons (405,027 liters) of water a year.

Land

What happens to all that garbage and trash? In one year the United States produces over 209 million tons of trash. Where does it all go? Doing something as simple as making a **compost** heap helps the land in many ways. Seven out of every ten pails of garbage can be made into compost.

You can make compost in your own backyard. You'll want to ask a parent first. Just mix leaves, grass clippings, old flowers and weeds with some dirt. You can also mix scraps of food. Turn the dirt pile each week with a shovel to give it some air. Add the compost to your garden or around bushes. Think of the rich soil you will be creating with garbage!

Here are other things you can do to cut down on garbage and trash and protect the land.

- When shopping, look for cereals, cookies, or other foods in packages made from recycled paper.
- Avoid excess packaging. Buy loose fruits and vegetables instead of those in plastic trays.
- Treat plants and trees with respect. Don't break off branches or strip off bark.
- Plant a tree. Trees help conserve soil and water.
- Take your plastic bags back to the grocery store. Use them again.
- Donate your old toys instead of throwing them out.

How can you help to conserve or protect our land?

A group of friends wearing T-shirts that spell out "Love Your Mother" pose in front of a model of Mother Earth.

Air

You can also take steps to keep the air clean and safe. Simple actions help keep our air clean.

Here are some ways you can help.

- Walk, ride your bike, or use public transportation instead of going by car.
- Don't smoke.
- Learn the safest way to dispose of hazardous waste materials such as old cans of paint, weed killers, or motor oil properly. Make sure that you or a family member doesn't toss them in the trash. Find a hazardous dump site in your area.
- Use pump sprays instead of aerosol cans.
- Research and share information about different ways of cleaning things naturally without using chemicals.

Many communities focus on clean air on Earth Day, an annual event each April. But you can create your own Clean Air Day. Pick a day with classmates or friends. Talk to the principal. Then others in school can take some action that will help keep the air clean. See how many people you can get to join in your Clean Air Day!

What will you do to help keep the air we breathe clean?

Reuse old things to make new things.

- Build a swing set out of old tires.
- Use glass jars to store things in.
- Use plastic soda bottles to grow plants or to store things.
- Write on both sides of your paper.
- Make jewelry using aluminum cans.
- Use old, torn clothes and towels to make rags.
- Turn used paper into note pads.

One item that is being discarded quickly are old computers. Computers are not good for landfills. Think how helpful to Earth it would be if people repaired and donated their computers.

Do you know people or groups in your community that fix old computers and donate them?

The 3 Rs

One of the best things that you can do to care for the Earth is to practice these 3 Rs—*reduce, recycle,* and *reuse*.

Reduce the amount of resources you use and the trash you create.

Recycle whenever you can. At home, help sort aluminum cans, glass, and newspapers into recycling bins for curbside pickup. When away from home, look for trash cans set aside for recyclables. Remember aluminum foil can also be recycled.

CHAPTER 4

Kids Take Action

If one person can make a difference, think how much more can get done if people work together to care for Planet Earth.

What can you and your friends do to help protect our Earth?

Kids Campaign Against Waste

Many kids and their classes are making a difference by paying attention to the packaging of the things they buy. Packaging includes all the stuff you throw away when you unwrap anything new.

One third of all trash is packaging. This is a big problem that will take time to solve. But each person can make a difference by becoming a smarter shopper.

On the left is the amount of trash an average family of four recycles in one year—about 1,100 pounds (499 kilograms). On the right is the amount of trash thrown away in one year—about 5,300 pounds (2,404 kilograms).

Mrs. Perez's 4th grade class decides to make their school and community aware of the waste in packaging. They want people to think before they buy. They also want to let the people who manufacture the products know that they want less waste in packaging. So they start an awareness campaign to help people change how they shop.

Class Project: Campaign Against Waste

1. Find out the facts. Use the Web to find out how much waste comes from packaging.
2. Go on a field trip to the mall. Take notes about how products, such as CDs, are packaged. Report on how much will be thrown away.
3. Read labels. Buy products that are in packages that can be recycled. Buy products that are made of recycled materials.
4. Say no to bags. If we don't need one, we don't use one.
5. Make posters to tell others what they can do.
6. Talk to our families and friends about what we learn.
7. Write class letters to the people who make our favorite products. Ask them to cut down on packaging.
8. Be patient. This is a big problem.

Another class decided to help save water. By working together they made a difference. Here's how they got started.

Miguel Salazar lives in Meridien, Texas. He is 11 years old and in the 4th grade. Every day he walks home from school and passes Carrolton Creek. The creek is filled with trash. Old tires, cardboard boxes, and broken branches from trees keep the water from flowing.

But the creek was not always this way. Miguel's grandfather remembers when the creek was beautiful. Flowers and plants grew along it. Many people fished there. Miguel would like to fish there again with his grandfather. He asks his class if they will help.

Miguel's 4th grade class decides to clean up the creek. They know conserving water is important. They make a plan.

Class Project: Creek Clean Up

1. Write a letter to the mayor asking her to let us have a clean-up day at Carrolton Creek. Ask her for garbage cans and help from the Sanitation Department to pick up recyclables.
2. Make posters inviting others to help.
3. Ask parents to come along and help on Clean-Up Day.
4. Ask stores to donate work gloves and garbage bags.
5. Choose a day for the big Clean Up!

Now it's your turn. You and your friends want to take action and make a difference. You want to do your part to help protect our natural resources.

But where and how do you start?

Here are some steps to help you get started.

Step 1: Identify the Problem

With your friends, identify some problems in your community. For example, do streams or ponds need to be cleaned up? Is your local park filled with litter? Does your family throw papers and glass out with the rest of the trash?

Model
Kinesha Thomas knew that there were things in her community she could do to help protect the Earth. Kinesha noticed that in the last year the park near her house was littered with paper cups, sandwich wrappers, and soda cans. The trash cans were always filled. She also remembered that the park was clean before a fast-food restaurant opened across the street.

Step 2: State the Problem

Once you and your friends have identified your problem, state what it is. Tell why it is a problem. List facts and information that help explain the problem.

Model
Kinesha knew that people bought food at the restaurant and liked to eat it in the park. Some people left their bags and soda cans on the benches. Others threw them in overflowing trash cans. The city collected the garbage twice a week. The park was a mess.

Step 3: Propose Solutions

List possible solutions to your problem. The solutions do not have to be in any order. You should have three or four different solutions if possible. You can find your solutions in books, on the Web, or by talking to people.

Model

Kinesha talked to her friends and listed different solutions to their problem. They thought about how they could prevent people from littering in the park. They interviewed people, visited other parks, and called the park district.

One solution was to ban eating and drinking in the park. Another was to fine anyone who littered. Another was to ask for more trash cans. A fourth solution was to ask the city to pick up the trash more often.

Step 4: Evaluate Solutions

Review your solutions. List the pros and cons of each solution. Take a vote among your friends for the best solution. Decide which one works best to solve your problem.

Model

Kinesha and her friends looked over their list of solutions. They decided that people liked eating in the park. They didn't want to ban this. They also thought that it would be hard to fine those who littered. A park guard would need to be there all the time. They thought that most people would use the trash cans if there were more of them. They also thought that they should be emptied more often.

Earth Watch

Every three months Americans throw away enough aluminum cans to rebuild our entire commercial airfleet.

When you have your solution, decide how you will present it. Think about the best way to share your problem and solution. When you have presented your problem and solution, people will be willing to help!

Model
Kinesha and her friends decided to hold a neighborhood meeting. They wrote a letter to the park district. They told how their park had changed in the last year. They asked for more trash cans. They also asked for more trash pickups each week. Their neighbors signed the letter. A small group met with the park district. They presented their request. Today the park is the clean, friendly place it used to be.

Kinesha and her friends succeeded. You can, too. You can do it! Work with your friends. Take action and solve a problem in your community!

Groups to Contact

Global Response Environmental Action & Education Network
Young Environmentalist's Action
http://www.globalresponse.org/yea/ideas.html
P.O. Box 7490
Boulder, CO 80306-7490
(303) 444-0306

Kids For a Clean Environment (F.A.C.E.)
http://www.kidsface.org/
P.O. Box 158254
Nashville, TN 37215
(615) 331-7381

Los Angeles County Department of Public Works
Generation Earth
http://www.generationearth.com/action/index.htm
(888) 3UP-2YOU

National Wildlife Federation
EarthSavers
http://www.nwf.org/earthsavers
11100 Wildlife Center Drive
Reston, VA 20190
(703) 438-6000

U.S. Environmental Protection Agency (EPA)
Explorers' Club
http://www.epa.gov/kids
Contact the regional office in your state.

Isaac Walton League of America
Young Ikes
http://www.iwla.org/yikes/
Outdoor America
707 Conservation Lane
Gaithersburg, MD 20878-2983

Glossary

acid rain rain or snow mixed with chemicals in the air from the burning of fuels

carbon dioxide colorless and odorless gas made up of carbon and oxygen

compost a mixture of decaying leaves, grass, or other matter used for fertilizing soil

conserve to keep from being wasted

cycle a series of events that keep coming back in the same order

deforestation removal of forests from land

economy a country's system for producing, distributing, and consuming goods, services, and resources

greenhouse effect the warming of Earth's surface

hydroelectric plant a factory that produces electricity by water power

irrigate to water land so it can produce crops

landfill a place where garbage is dumped

manufacture to make goods, by hand or machine, usually in large quantities

natural resource anything supplied by nature that is useful or necessary for life

nonrenewable resource a natural resource that is limited in supply and cannot be replaced

nutrient a substance found in food that is needed for growth of humans, plants, and animals

oxygen a colorless, odorless, and tasteless gas needed by all living things

ozone layer the thin layer of gas in the atmosphere that protects life on Earth

pesticide a poison used to kill weeds, insects, etc.

polluting making dirty or impure

renewable resource a natural resource that can be replaced for use later

Index

acid rain 17
air 4, 5, 6, 7, 8, 11, 13, 14, 21,
carbon dioxide 11
compost 20
conservation 6, 19, 20, 26
deforestation 16
drought 18
earthquakes 18
economy 8
fertilizers 14
floods 18
greenhouse effect 15
hydroelectric plants 8
industries 8
irrigate 8
land 4, 5, 6, 7, 8, 10, 13, 14, 20
landfills 17

natural disasters 18
nutrients 10
oxygen 11
oxygen-carbon dioxide cycle 11
ozone layer 16
pesticides 14
pollution 12, 13, 14
recycling 22
resources
    natural, 4, 5, 6, 7, 27
    nonrenewable, 5
    renewable, 5
soil 10
trash 17, 20
waste 15, 25
water 4, 5, 6, 7, 8, 9,13, 14, 19,
water cycle 9